WITHDRAWAL

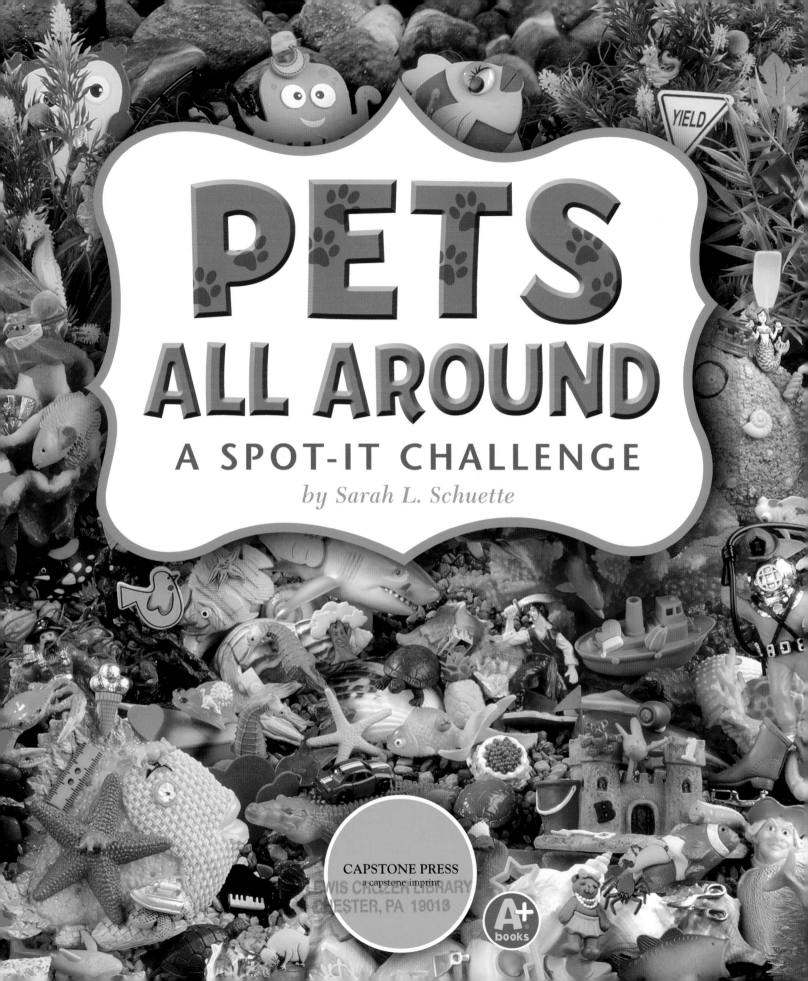

PETS
ALL AROUND
A SPOT-IT CHALLENGE

by Sarah L. Schuette

CAPSTONE PRESS
a capstone imprint

A+
books

A+ Books are published by Capstone Press,
1710 Roe Crest Drive, North Mankato, Minnesota 56003.
www.capstonepub.com

Library of Congress Cataloging-in-Publication Data
Schuette, Sarah, L., 1976–
Pets All Around: A Spot-It Challenge / by Sarah L. Schuette
p. cm (A+ Books. Spot it.)
Summary: "Simple text invites the reader to find items hidden in pet-themed
photographs"—Provided by publisher.
ISBN 978-1-4296-8713-3 (library binding)
ISBN 978-1-62065-199-5 (eBook PDF)
1. Picture puzzles—juvenile literature. 2. Pets—juvenile literature. I. Title. II. Series.
GV1507.P47 S3776 2013
793.73—dc23   2012019499

Credits
Jeni Wittrock, editor; Juliette Peters, designer; Jo Miller, media researcher; Laura Manthe,
    production specialist; Sarah Schuette, photo stylist; Marcy Morin, photo scheduler

Photo Credits
All photos by Capstone Studio: Karon Dubke

The author dedicates this book to her cousin, Josie Schmidt.

Note to Parents, Teachers, and Librarians
Spot It is an interactive series that supports literacy development and reading enjoyment.
Readers utilize visual discrimination skills to find objects among fun-to-peruse photographs
with busy backgrounds. Readers also build vocabulary through thematic groupings,
develop visual memory ability through repeated readings, and improve strategic and
associative thinking skills by experimenting with different visual search methods.

Printed in the United States of America in North Mankato, Minnesota.
042012   006682CGF12

Table of Contents

Pet Store

Can you spot ...

- a hammer?
- a ferret?
- a brush?
- a lion?
- an elephant?
- a banana bunch?

5

Cats

Can you spot ...

- a cactus?
- a snowflake?
- a castle?
- a lobster?
- a tomato?
- a steak?

Birds

Can you spot ...
- a laptop?
- two skateboards?
- a strawberry?
- a tugboat?
- a spoon?
- a teddy bear?

Hamsters

Can you spot ...

- a swan?
- a whistle?
- a pineapple?
- a dragon?
- a fried egg?
- a unicorn?

11

Fish

Can you spot …

- a Band Aid?
- a surfboard?
- a taco?
- a mitten?
- a lantern?
- a jellyfish?

Turtle Party

Can you spot …

- a robot?
- a guitar?
- a pretzel?
- a jet ski?
- a zebra?
- a drum?

14

15

Mealtime!

Can you spot ...
- a pinecone?
- a pumpkin?
- a crown?
- a key?
- a spoon?
- two cupcakes?

17

Pet Rocks

Can you spot …

- a purse?
- a cat?
- two teddy bears?
- a sheep?
- a police car?
- a bowling pin?

19

Hermits

Can you spot …
- a panda?
- a pig?
- a donut?
- a clothespin?
- a football?
- a flip-flop?

Dogs

Can you spot ...
- a toothbrush?
- a milk jug?
- a sun?
- a goldfish?
- a teapot?
- a horse?

Spiders

Can you spot ...
- a trumpet?
- a notebook?
- a tent?
- an acorn?
- a tennis racket?
- a hand?

Vet

Can you spot …
- a sandwich?
- a ghost?
- a rubber band?
- two baseballs?
- a maple leaf?
- a domino?

FAVORITE DOGS

Spot Even More!

Pet Store 4

Try to spot a pair of glasses, an ice-cream cone, a golf tee, three loaves of French bread, and a scissors.

Cats 6

This time find two cherries, a hat, a head of cabbage, an ice-cream bar, a whisk, and a basketball.

Birds 8

Now look for an ear of corn, two shamrocks, a bunch of grapes, and the letter "A."

Hamsters 10

Take another look to find a school bus, a princess, a pitchfork, a bluebird, and a ladder.

Fish 12

Time to find a saxophone, a fishing pole, an umbrella, a pencil sharpener, and a bowl of potato chips.

Turtle Party 14

Now spot a grill, a bathtub, a giraffe, a sea horse, and a dustpan.

Mealtime!

See if you can find a hermit crab, a playground slide, a lamp, and a traffic cone.

Pet Rocks

Check for a Christmas tree, a satellite, a set of golf clubs, and the letter "L."

Hermits

See if you can spot a paintbrush, a dragonfly, a treasure chest, and a tennis shoe.

Dogs

Try to find a seal, a slice of watermelon, a dolphin, and a piece of bread.

Spiders

Try to find an astronaut, the Statue of Liberty, a sea turtle, a pencil, and a mousetrap.

Vet

See if you can spot a pair of overalls, a slice of pizza, two flowerpots, and a dodo bird.

Extreme Spot-It Challenge

Just can't get enough Spot-It action?
Here's an extra challenge. Try to spot:

- a rainbow
- two erasers
- a pair of ballet slippers
- a teacup
- a tennis ball
- a Christmas bulb
- a safari hat
- a roller skate
- two sand buckets
- a motorcycle
- a bundle of wood
- a ponytail holder
- a tube of lipstick
- two popsicles
- a black dress
- a hot dog
- a magic wand

Read More

Chedru, Delphine. *Spot It Again!: Find More Hidden Creatures.* New York: Abrams Books for Young Readers, 2011.

Marks, Jennifer L. *Fun and Games: A Spot-It Challenge.* Spot It. Mankato, Minn.: Capstone Press, 2009.

Schuette, Sarah L. *Animal Fun: A Spot-It Challenge.* Spot It. Mankato, Minn.: Capstone Press, 2012.

Internet Sites

FactHound offers a safe, fun way to find Internet sites related to this book. All of the sites on FactHound have been researched by our staff.

Here's all you do:

Visit *www.facthound.com*

Type in this code: **9781429687133**

Super-cool stuff! Check out projects, games and lots more at www.capstonekids.com